FOREWORD

Using websites is becoming more and more popular, small businesses are getting online, and we live in a world where information is freely available on web pages.

We are now selling our used clothes on eBay. We are ordering our food through Amazon, and the rise of technology usage have reached the sky.

Customers are now looking for information online, buying online, communication online, dating online. This makes the web a hot area where businesses try to attract new customers.

People type billions of queries into Google search bar to find relevant information or buy products, and in order to get a market share from the Google's search traffic, you will need to rank your website mainly in the first page. In the result, new terms like search engine optimization (SEO) pops out, and become an new billion dollar industry.

This is the rise of SEO: free organic traffic has a huge potential to make billions of dollars for businesses and industries.

SEOs, webmasters or just self-made entrepreneurs are using black hat ways to hack Google to rank their websites even if the quality is poor, or their websites are non-relevant.

So, Google is tweaking their search algorithm to bring down websites made by black hat communities, making them losing billions and billions of dollars.

Google is incorporating 200+ search ranking factors to determine if a website deserve to be ranked or not. But, if you play by the rules and follow their webmaster guidelines, your websites will never be impacted by their future algorithm updates.

That is the goal of this book. Teaching you **the only 72 Google's search ranking factors that you need to focus on and optimize for**, in order o rank your website in the first page of Google search results.

Those are exactly the ranking factors we use to rank all our WordPress website.

TABLE OF CONTENTS

LISTE DES FIGURES

CHAPTER I

About WordPress

Introduction

WordPress is a free and open source CMS[1] that was built mainly for blogging, and becomes after that widely used for different use cases such as websites, corporate websites, forum application, affiliate platform, games, and all things web.

WordPress is based on the PHP and database. It's a dynamic CMS, we called this PHP websites. All the posts, pages, images are stored in a database.

1.1. WordPress Strengths

WordPress is a flexible CMS that you can use for blogs, build websites, run a network of websites, and has a wide variety of **themes** and **plugins** which make it a choice when it comes to choose on which platform you will build your next dream website.

1.1.1. WordPress Themes

WordPress has its own marketplace for themes which combines both free and paid themes. You can also choose an external marketplace like ThemeForest for your new website's theme or just buy from a reputable WordPress web design company like ElegantThemes which I use personally for all my personal and corporate websites www.hostgarou.com.

---

[1] Content Management System

1.1.2. WordPress Plugins

WordPress has its own marketplace for plugins which combines both free and paid plugins. You can also choose some external marketplaces for your new website's plugin or just buy from reputable developers or a development companies. Most of the web developers out there offer both free and paid versions of their plugins, if you want some extra features that comes with their free plugin, go for their paid plugins.

1.2. WordPress Philosophy and Benefits

WordPress has many advantages over other paid CMS for blog and websites, some of which are listed below:

Open source

The license agreement of WordPress respects the open-source ideology, you can at any time download the source code and modify it according to you tastes. WordPress uses powerful open-sources libraries for databases, images uploads, file management, etc.

Free

Wordpress.org is free to use for unlimited websites or blogs for life. However, there is a paid version of WordPress which is at wordpress.com and owned by the company behind WordPress development.

Easy to develop

WordPress is made for simplicity, you can use its API[2] which accelerate the development workflow and enable you to crack down its core base in no time.

You can also build free or paid plugins for WordPress, WordPress themes, or use the API to connect your application or your websites with the WordPress system.

Easy to sell

According to trusted sources, WordPress is powering nearly 30% of all the web, which create a huge demand of all WordPress related things. You can sell plugins, themes, WordPress security, consulting, etc.

Flexible

The WordPress system is extremely flexible, with responsive themes, it adapts to many different plateforms, like smartphones, tablets, PCs, etc...

Not only it is a huge chance to have so many opportunities, but WordPress is built to facilitate development and distribution depending on the components present in the core which make it an obvious choice for many companies for their internal and future projects.

---

[2] Application Programming Interface.

CHAPTER II

WordPress SEO

Introduction

Before digging into WordPress SEO, you will need at least have the basic knowledge of what is SEO? How you can do SEO? Why do you need SEO?

Let's focus now on the word SEO.

SEO means search engine optimization. It's the art of optimizing a website or a blog to be search engine friendly.

The "WordPress SEO" term has no difference from just the "SEO" term, since both means basically the same thing which is SEO. But WordPress SEO is slightly more difficult and I will tell you why! To answer this question, let's first pop up the HTML websites term and compares it to a WordPress website.

WordPress is:

- Running on a database, which requires more speed optimization vs. HTML website which does not.
- WordPress has different link structures like posts, pages, categories, tags, taxonomies, and dynamically generated content which requires a sort of automation to be able to optimize for SEO, unlike HTML which is very easy with its simple ".html" URLs structure.

You understand now why we call it "WordPress SEO"? All right, let's dig right into it.

In this chapter, you will learn all the strategies we use to optimize a WordPress website for SEO, and the different hacks to rank it on the search results like Google, which the primary source of traffic for all websites. Things are getting serious here, are you ready?

We will divide the SEO into 2 separate part:

- **On-Page WordPress SEO:** this means that SEO is focused on the website optimization aspect, we will work ON the page, posts, CMS, etc. This is where we will focus our efforts.
- **Off-Page WordPress SEO:** this is more about general SEO and not related by any means to WordPress SEO. General SEO will work for all kind of websites or blogs, but this is also by far the most important aspect of ranking a website in Google and other search engines.

In this book, we will focus on the only search engine that matter for all of us, Google! Why?

Well, because Google sends quality traffic and it's like a monopoly in information and product based traffic. Look at your Google Analytics and your traffic sources. Do you see nearly 90% of traffic coming just from Google? You have now your answer!

Let's move on and show you the results we are able to achieve using the technics and strategies that I am going to teach you in this WordPress SEO book.

2.1. WordPress SEO Results

To give this book more credibility. I would like to show you first some of the results that we were able to achieve to rank some WordPress websites, and get more genuine and organic traffic from it.

For this, I will use our corporate website www.hostgarou.com and www.hostgarou.ma and how I was able to rank it for very competitive keywords.

1. Keywords 1: "hebergement web maroc"
2. Keywords 2: "web hosting free trial"

I will not expose all the keywords I choose to rank on the page one number one position on Google to avoid the competition, but this will give you largely more motivation to keep reading this book.

Please note that results may change if Google updates their algorithm, at the time of writing this book which September 24, 2017, we were ranked for those keywords at:

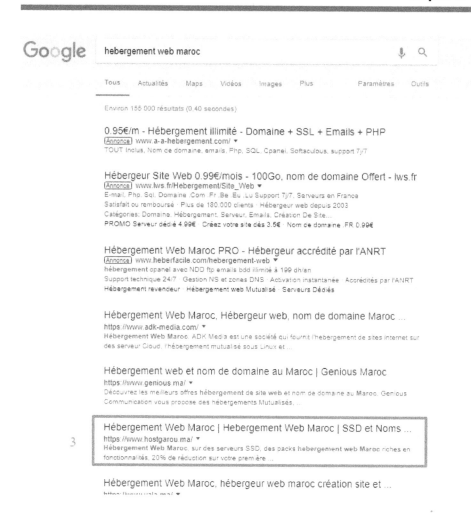

Figure 1. Keyword 1: "hebergement web maroc", Date : 24 September 2017

Figure Analysis:

From over 155.000 search results we are ranked number 3 on the first page on Google. There are 155.000 websites on all over the web competing for this keyword, or at least talking about this topic. But Google trust us more and rank our website for this search query.

Google — Web Hosting Free Trial

Tous Actualités Vidéos Images Plus   Paramètres Outils

Environ 4 040 000 résultats (0,25 secondes)

Web Hosting Free Trial - Pickaweb
https://www.pickaweb.co.uk/free-trial/ ▾ Traduire cette page
Try our web hosting services for FREE & see why 20000 UK Small Businesses Trust Pickaweb. 30
days free hosting trial.

Web hosting sign-up with 30 day FREE Trial
https://www.virtualempire.com/ordernow/ ▾ Traduire cette page
Sign up for Web hosting. ... Free Trial offered on Shared Hosting plans only ... Register a new website
name. I have a domain name and want to use VE hosting.

Free cPanel Web Hosting Trial | Best Free Hosting in Australia
https://www.netregistry.com.au/web-hosting/free-trial/ ▾ Traduire cette page
Try cPanel web hosting free for 1 month. Linux powered running Apache our cPanel hosting boasts
lightning speed, performance and unmatched reliability.

2 months of free web hosting | ONEbit hosting
https://www.onebit.cz/en/webhosting-zdarma/ ▾ Traduire cette page
2 months of ONEbit hosting for free. Don't pay anything for the trial period. Really.

Website Builder Free Trial - Name.com
https://www.name.com/website-builder-free-trial ▾ Traduire cette page
With Name.com's Website Builder, it's easy to create a sleek and professional website for your
business. Free 14 day trial!

7 Best Free Trial Web Hosting Sites In 2017 (NO CREDIT CARD)
https://roadtoblogging.com/free-trial-hosting/ ▾ Traduire cette page
Looking for a free trial hosting? Check our list of 7 best free trial web hosting sites for 2017. You don't
need to add your credit card to use services.

Free Trial - Bluehost
https://www.bluehost.com/trial_disclaimer.html ▾ Traduire cette page
bluehost - professional web hosting ... You will not be charged until the end of your 30-day free trial. ...
Our money-back guarantee applies to hosting plans, but does not apply to most add-on products, such
as domains, given the unique nature ...

Web Hosting Free Trial For 15 days - Free Trial SSD Hosting
https://www.hostgarou.com/web-hosting-free-trial/ ▾ Traduire cette page
Web hosting free trial with instant activation, with rich features and no obligation, we have fastest SSD
servers, we offer the best hosting here. Order now.

8

Figure 2. Keyword 2: "web hosting free trial", Date: 24 September 2017

Figure Analysis:

From over 4.040.000 search results we are ranked number 8 on the first page on Google. There are 4.040.000 websites on all over the web competing for this keyword, or at least talking about this topic. But Google trust us more and rank our website for this search query.

Pretty amazing result, right? And we are not far from position number one for these queries which receive decent amount of traffic.

These are proofs that the technics I teach in this book are working very well.

SEO becomes irrelevant and technics becomes outdated by the time Google is tweaking their algorithm. At the time of writing this book, September 2017, information in this book is up-to-date with industry changes. Feel free to use them.

But wait, how can you rank a website in Google while you don't even know what Google takes into consideration when he wants to rank a website?

Those consideration are called search ranking factors. And I am going to introduce you to these guys.

Google uses more than 200 search ranking factors when it comes on whether to rank a website number one, two, three, four, five, etc.

CHAPTER III

72 Google Search Ranking Factors (2017)

Remember, you are on a mission to rank your website higher in the search results, don't play black hat and always play white hat. If you play by the Google's rules you will always win.

These are the only 72 search ranking factors that Google is using, and you will need to focus on to rank a website, and here are all of them:

3.1. Domain Specific Ranking Factors

1. Keyword appearing in SLD:

Let me explain this first, a domain name like google.com = SLD.TLD

- TLD: Top Level Domain
- SLD: Second Level Domain

This ranking factor used to give a ranking boost, but you want your website to be relevant to searchers, so make sure to include your main keyword in your SLD.

2. Domain history:

If you have a domain name with several registrar drops, it will impact your SEO efforts and backlinks pointing to this domain name, and tell Google to "reset" the domain's history.

3. Old domain names:

Matt Cutts said that:

"The difference between a domain that's six months old versus one-year old is really not that big at all."

From my personal experience, I saw that domain age plays a big role in search ranking. To prove this, just "google", the verb, a keyword and check results one by one. You will notice that only aged domains that popped up in the first 5 positions in the 1 first page.

4. A domain name with the keyword at first, left area:

If you put your keyword at the start of your domain name, it will get more weight from Google over a domain that have the keyword in the middle, end or don't have this keyword.

5. Exact match domain:

You will get an extra boost with exact match domains only if it is a quality website. But, if the exact match domain is a low-quality website, it's may cost you low rankings.

 Matt Cutts ✓
@mattcutts

Minor weather report: small upcoming Google algo change will reduce low-quality "exact-match" domains in search results.

3:43 PM - 28 Sep 12 - Embed this Tweet

6. ccTLD domains:

Getting a Country Code Top Level Domain (like .us, .br. de, .in, etc.) will get your website to rank in that specific country, it's guaranteed, but will impact the domain's ability to rank globally. You can find this option under your Google WebMaster Console Tools, and target a country with your domain of choice.

3.2. Page-Level Specific Ranking Factors

7. Keywords in title tag:

Make sure to include your main keyword in your title tag, because it is considered by Google the most important ranking factor following quality website content. Hence, it will boost your On-Page SEO.

8. Title tag starting with keyword:

Title tags starting with the target keyword (left side) ranks better in search engines rather a title tag with this keyword at the end of the title tag:

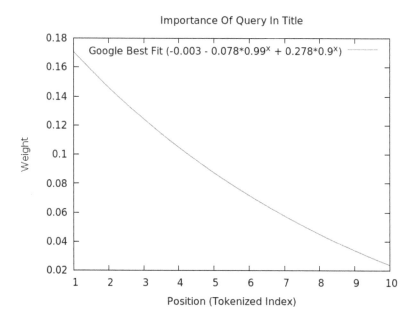

9. Keyword in the description tag:

Make sure to include your keyword at the start of your description tag, Google is still bolding keywords in the search results.

10. Keyword appears in H1 tag:

Make sure to include your keyword at the start of your H1 tag, this will send a relevancy signal to Google that the content in your page/post is about that topic.

11. Keyword in H2, H3 Tags:

Make sure to include your keyword at the start of your H2/H3/H4 tag, this will send a relevancy signal to Google that the content in your page/post is about that topic.

12. Keyword density or frequency:

Make sure to mention your targeted keyword multiple times in your pages/posts.

13. Content length:

Longer content performs better in search results and ranks higher. Make sure the quality of your content is good, and include at least 1.000 words in your pages/posts.

14. Page load speed

Make sure to optimize your page load speed, faster webpages rank higher in search results.

Use a tool called GTMetrix to get an idea on how fast your website is.

15. Rel = Canonical:

Use *rel = canonical* tag in all your webpages to prevent Google from penalizing your site due to duplicate content.

16. Image ALT tag:

Make sure to include your keyword in your image alt tag. This will send a strong signal to Google that this page with its content is all about that topic.

17. Updated content:

Google has updated their algorithm to favor recently updated content, and hence rank I higher in search results. Google includes updated time in the results.

What Is A Backlink and How Do You Start Getting Backlinks To Your ...

.../backlink.html ▾

Jul 16, 2017 **Backlinks** are incoming links to a webpage. When a webpage links to any other page, it's called a **backlink**. In the past, **backlinks** were the major metric for the ranking of a webpage. A page with a lot of **backlinks** tended to rank higher on all major search engines, including Google.

18. Keyword prominence:

Make sure to include your page's main keyword in the first 100 words, it will send a strong relevancy signal to Google.

19. Outbound link quality:

Send strong trust signal to Google by including outbound links to authority websites.

20. Number of internal links pointing to a page:

Make sure to link internally to your most important webpages. This will indicate how important is this page and result in higher search ranking.

21. Keyword in URL:

Google is still bolding keywords in URLs, so make sure to include keywords in your pages URL. This an important relevancy signal.

3.3. WebSite-Level Factors

22. Website architecture:

Make sure to organize architecturally your website in simple manner by categories to help Google better understand your niche.

23. Presence of Sitemap:

Build your website sitemap, and send it to Google, Bing, Yahoo, and other search engines. This will index your new content faster and rank it better.

24. Website uptime:

Make sure to keep 100% monthly server uptime, otherwise, downtime will hurt your search engine ranking and may result in your website deindexing. Visit www.hostgarou.com and get an SSD hosting for your website. SSDs are more known for their 100% monthly uptime, since they have no mechanical parts that may fail. Resulting in much more guaranteed uptime.

25. Secure HTTP or HTTPS:

Google confirm in their WebMaster Blog that they index HTTPS websites and give them a ranking boost.

26. Terms of service and privacy policy web pages:

Make sure to publish these two pages, this tells Google that a site is a trustworthy member of the web community.

27. Responsive websites or mobile-friendly sites:

I can't stress enough to tell how important to have a responsive website, which adapt to all screen sizes in a mobile world. This will get your website a ranking boost with mobile searchers.

Otherwise, Google will decrease the visibility of your website in search. This a major ranking factor. So please contact you web designer and ask for help.

28. User reviews and weSite reputation:

Get your website listed on Yelp and Google for Business, ask your visitors for reviews and watch your ranking.

3.4. Backlinks Ranking Factors

29. Links from old domains:

Getting backlinks from old domains have more value than getting them from new domains.

30. The number of linking root domains:

The more the number of domain linking to your domain, the more you get higher in search results. This by far the most important Google ranking factor.

Moz (bottom axis is SERP position):

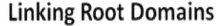

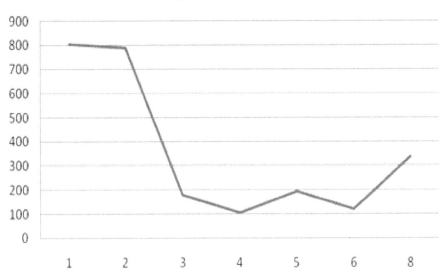

31. Backlinks from .edu and .gov domains:

SEO industry thinks that getting links from .edu and .org domain may boost the ranking.

32. Authority of linking page:

This is one of the most important ranking factor, authority (PageRank) web pages linking with you gives you more ranking juice.

33. Authority of linking domain:

This is one of the most important ranking factor, authority domains linking with you give you more ranking juice, and better positions in the search results.

34. Social shares of linking pages:

If the page linking with your domain gets lots of social shares, it will get more Google's value and weight, and for instance, impacting your search ranking.

35. Guest posts:

Guest posting is a white hat link building tactic, write valuable content and distribute it in websites similar to your niche.

36. ccTLd referring domains:

Make sure to get links from your local industry, if you have for example a .uk website, you will need hunt for a backlink from .uk domains, this will send Google a signal that you are active in your country, and hence rank you higher in your local area.

37. Linking domain relevancy:

Getting a backlink from similar websites in your niche send Google strong signal about your website relevancy and result in higher ranking.

38. Page link relevancy:

Getting a backlink from similar page in your niche send Google strong signal about your web page relevancy and result in higher ranking.

39. Keyword in title:

Google gives more weight to links on pages that include your web page's main keyword in title.

40. Backlinks from authority websites:

Getting a link from authority website like forbes.com or cnn.com passes more search ranking juice to your website.

41. Links from Wikipedia:

Even if those links are "nofollow", but Google loves to see a Wikipedia page linking with your domain name.

42. Old backlinks:

Google loves old backlinks, they show that a website is authentic and more established than newly created backlinks.

43. Natural link profile:

A website with naturel link profile will standout against Google's dance and their future Penguin or Panda updates.

44. Google Rich Snippet:

Web pages that support Google Rich Snippet ranks higher in search results, and have higher CTR.

Camera - Chrome Web Store
https://chrome.google.com/webstore/.../camera/hfhhnacclhffhdffklopdkcgdhifgngh?h... ▼
★★★✩ ⋆ Rating: 3.4 - 3,430 votes - Free - Chrome - Entertainment
An easy-to-use Camera app for taking hilarious photos! By installing this item, you agree to the Google Terms of Service and Privacy Policy at ...

45. Thin linking Content:

A backlink from 1500-word count post has more value than 100-word count post.

46. Quality of Linking Content:

Getting backlinks from poorly written content may decrease search engine rankings.

3.5. User Interaction

47. Organic high CTR:

Search results links that are getting lots of clicks get high *Click Through Rate*, resulting in higher ranking.

48. Bounce Rate:

Go check your Google Analytics, and if you found that your website's visitors bounce quickly, you may want tot try to keep them a lot more in your website. Google uses this data to determine if this search result respond to their visitor's queries. If it is yes, they rank it higher, if not they rank it lower.

49. Repeated traffic:

Google uses also returning visitors metrics under their Analytics to find our if their visitors are returning to visit those websites again, and may rank them higher.

50. Comments count:

If a page gets lots of engaging comments, this sends Google a good quality signal.

51. Dwell time:

If Google visitors spend lots of time on your web pages, Google love that and may reward your site in search results.

3.6. Special Algorithm Rules

52. Transactional searches:

Google returns different search results for transactional queries like booking a hotel.

53. Local searches:

Google often display Google Business Places above ordinary search results, and sometimes below them.

54. Google News Box:

Google sometimes favor their News, and display their News Box above normal results.

55. Google RankBrain

Google use a machine learning system to help them process billions of search queries. This artificial intelligence is just a part of Google algorithm. We don't know too much about it, but we know that AI is constantly learning and tweaking itself like a human.

3.7. Social Signals

56. Number of Twitter Tweets:

Links that are getting lots of tweets rank better in search results.

57. Facebook Likes:

Links that are getting lots of Facebook likes rank better in search results.

58. Facebook Shares:

Links that are getting lots of Facebook shares rank better in search results.

59. Pinterest Pins:

Links that are getting lots of Pinterest Pins rank better in search results.

60. Votes on social sharing websites:

Google uses websites like Digg, Reddit, Stumbleupon as a ranking factor.

3.8. Brand Signals

61. Brand name anchor text:

Google uses brand names anchor text as a strong brand signal.

62. Branded searches:

If visitors type your "brand name + keyword" or just the brand name in the search box, Google knows that is a genuine brand.

63. Facebook page:

Brands that have a Facebook page with lots of fans is a strong signal for Google that this is an authentic brand.

64. Twitter profile:

Brands that have a Twitter Profile with lots of follower is a strong signal for Google that this is an authentic brand.

65. LinkedIn company page:

Brands that have a LinkedIn company page with lots of follower is a strong signal for Google that this is an authentic brand.

66. Brand citations:

Google is able to catch brand that get mentioned in social networks without getting linked to. This sends Google a brand signal.

3.9. On-Page Web Spam Ranking Factors

67. Panda penalty:

Thin or low-quality content (particularly content farms) are less visible in search results. Panda will hit hard on that.

68. Cloaking:

Serving your visitors different results than they expected is against Google TOS. You will be penalized for this if caught and get your website complexly deindexed.

69. Ads above the fold:

Make sure to put ads below the fold, or the "<u>Page Layout Algorithm</u>" will penalize your website, if lots of your ads (and not much content) are above the fold.

3.10. Off-Page Web Spam Ranking Factors

70. Link profile with high percentage of low quality links:

Getting lots of links from sources like social profiles, forum profiles, or blog comment with no value may penalize your website in the search.

71. Linking domain relevancy:

A SEO website guy found that websites with an unnaturally high amount of backlinks from unrelated websites were more vulnerable to Google Penguin Penalty.

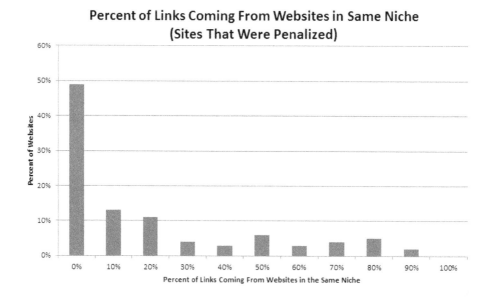

72. Links from the same class C IPs:

If you are getting lots of backlinks from websites on the same server IP, this may be a signal of Private Blog Network or PBN.

CONCLUSION

It is actually clear that organic traffic converts better that paid traffic, and this privilege is not given to anyone.

The SEO war will never ends, and even if Google is pushing extremely down websites utilizing black hat technics, black hat has taken new forms of white hat technics, and Google may never will able to take them all down.

But the new Google RankBrain AI may a day be able to achieve what human is being able to do.

Resume

Using websites is becoming more and more popular, small businesses are getting online, and we live in a world where information is freely available on web pages.

We are now selling our used clothes on eBay. We are ordering our food through Amazon, and the rise of technology usage have reached the sky.

Customers are now looking for information online, buying online, communication online, dating online. This makes the web a hot area where businesses try to attract new customers.

People type billions of queries into Google search bar to find relevant information or buy products, and in order to get a market share from the Google's search traffic, you will need to rank your website mainly in the first page. In the result, new terms like search engine optimization (SEO) pop out, and become an new billion dollar industry.

This is the rise of SEO: free organic traffic has a huge potential to make billions of dollars for businesses and industries.

SEOs, webmasters or just self-made entrepreneurs are using black hat ways to hack Google to rank their websites even if the quality is poor, or their websites are non-relevant.

So, Google is tweaking their search algorithm to bring down websites made by black hat communities, making them losing billions and billions of dollars.

Google is incorporating 200 + search ranking factors in order to determine if a website deserve to be ranked or not. But, if you play by the rules and follow their webmaster guidelines, your websites will never be impacted by their future algorithm updates.

That is the goal of this book. Teaching you **the only 72 Google's search ranking factors that you need to focus on and optimize for**, in order o rank your website in the first page of Google search results.

Those are exactly the ranking factors we use to rank all our WordPress website.

www.ingramcontent.com/pod-product-compliance
Lightning Source LLC
LaVergne TN
LVHW052324060326
832902LV00023B/4586